Nita Mehta's
MICROWAVE
Vegetarian Cookery

Nita Mehta

B.Sc. (Home Science), M.Sc. (Food and Nutrition), Gold Medalist

Co author
Harveen Choudhary

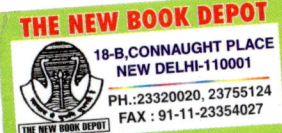

SNAB Publishers Pvt Ltd

D1694871

Nita Mehta's
MICROWAVE
VEGETARIAN COOKERY

© Copyright 2002-2007 **SNAB** Publishers Pvt Ltd

WORLD RIGHTS RESERVED. The contents—all recipes, photographs and drawings are original and copyrighted. No portion of this book shall be reproduced, stored in a retrieval system or transmitted by any means, electronic, mechanical, photocopying, recording or otherwise, without the written permission of the publishers.

While every precaution is taken in the preparation of this book, the publisher and the author assume no responsibility for errors or omissions. Neither is any liability assumed for damages resulting from the use of information contained herein.

TRADEMARKS ACKNOWLEDGED. Trademarks used, if any, are acknowledged as trademarks of their respective owners. These are used as reference only and no trademark infringement is intended upon.

15th Print 2008
ISBN 978-81-86004-19-7

Food Styling and Photography: **SNAB**

Layout and laser typesetting :

N.I.T.A.
☎ 23252948

National Information
Technology Academy
3A/3, Asaf Ali Road
New Delhi-110002

Contributing Writers :
Anurag Mehta
Subhash Mehta

Editorial & Proofreading :
Rakesh
Ramesh

Distributed by :
THE VARIETY BOOK DEPOT
A.V.G. Bhavan, M 3 Con Circus,
New Delhi - 110 001
Tel : 23417175, 23412567; Fax : 23415335
Email: varietybookdepot@rediffmail.com

Printed by :
BRIJBASI ART PRESS LTD.

Published by :
SNAB
Publishers Pvt. Ltd.
3A/3 Asaf Ali Road,
New Delhi - 110002
Tel: 23252948, 23250091
Telefax:91-11-23250091

Editorial and Marketing office:
E-159, Greater Kailash-II, N.Delhi-48
Fax: 91-11-29225218, 29229558
Tel: 91-11-29214011, 29218727, 29218574
E-Mail: nitamehta@email.com
nitamehta@nitamehta.com
Website: http://www.nitamehta.com
Website: http://www.snabindia.com

Rs. 89/-

All the recipes are well tried and perfect

Bake a perfect cake in just 4 minutes!

Microwave a quick snack for unexpected guests!

Delicious Indian foods can be served in no time!

Microwave ovens can cook Continental & Chinese dishes too!

Round off your meals with desserts which can be microwaved within a few minutes!

Note: *Ther term 'micro high' means that the dish is to be microwaved at 100% power which is the normal way to microwave.*

Introduction

Say good-bye to long hours in the kitchen. With the help of your microwave, prepare great tasting recipes in the shortest possible time.

Microwave leaves most foods tastier, retains the natural and fresh colour of food . There is no danger of food sticking to the bottom of your pan and getting burnt. An added advantage is that you can cook with very little oil. Cook, reheat and serve in the same dish and therefore, there is less washing up to do.

However, microwave cooking is a little different from conventional cooking. This book shall help you to actually cook the food in a microwave & get your moneys worth.

I am sure you will enjoy using this book.

Happy Microwaving!

Contents

SNACKS 13
- Potato Based Pizza 14
- Paneer Tikka 16
- Khandavi 18
- Dlightful Paneer with Grapes 22
- Masala Idli 24
- Potato Chaat 26

INDIAN MAIN DISHES 27
- Mushroom & Capsicum Bhujia 28
- Zayekedar Arbi 32
- Corn Korma 34
- Saunf ke Karele 36
- Rasmise Aloo Matar 38

Kati Bhindi 40
Kadhai Paneer 41
Navratan Korma 42
Khoya Matar 44
Bharvaan Baingan 46
Paneer Hara Pyaz 49
Paneer Makhani 50
Makhani Korma 52
Mixed Masala Subzi 54
Stir fried Baby Corns 56
Spinach & Carrot Rice 58
Matar Wale Chaawal 60
Sukhi Dhuli Urad Dal 62

CONTINENTAL MAIN DISHES 63
Sauted Mushrooms 64

Stuffed Tomatoes 68
Macaroni Cheese 70
Corn & Cheese in Mustard Sauce 72
Mushroom Fondue 74

DESSERTS 75
Stewed Peaches in Sauce 76
Benarasi Kheer 78
Phirni 80
Nutty Mango Sauce 82
Mango Bread Pudding 86
Gajar ka Halwa 88

CAKES 89
Chocolate Walnut Cake 90
Basic Vanilla Cake 92

Important Tips for using Microwave

- The golden rule for microwaving is never to over cook food. You can always microwave the under cooked food for a few more minutes, but an over cooked food tends to become dry and hard.

- Use china (bone china or ordinary china), glass or pyrex dishes. Metal (stainless steel) dishes are not micro proof. Plastic may be used only for reheating and not for cooking.

- Never use dishes for microwaving that have gold or silver (metal) lines.

- Do not use delicate glass as this may crack due to the heat from the food.

- Never attempt to cover with aluminium foil. However cling film can be used for short cooking durations. Cover with an ordinary full plate

Potato based Pizza : page 14

of ordinary china if you do not have a lid for the dish. Do not use a melmoware plate to cover for long periods while microwaving.

- Do not use a plastic container when cooking time exceeds 5 minutes. The shape of the container may get distorted.

- Use wooden kebab sticks instead of metal skewers.

- Use deep dishes to prepare gravies, filling the dish only ¾ full. Gravies may spill otherwise. Take big, flat dishes, about 1"-2" height to prepare dry vegetables.

- Milk based foods tend to boil over so a larger and deeper container should be used to prevent spilling.

- All liquids should be stirred mid-way during cooking/heating to ensure uniform cooking/heating.

- The colder the food, the longer it takes to heat up. Food from a fridge takes longer to reheat/cook than food at room temperature.

Sukhi Dhuli Urad Dal : page 62

- Never pile food on top of each other. It cooks better, evenly & quickly when spaced apart.

- Food cooks better in a round container than in a square one, although you may use dishes of any shape that you posses.

- A little standing time should be given to the cooked food, because the cooking process continues for a while even after the microwave is switched off.

- When baking cakes, the cake batter has to be much thinner than the ordinary batter. Add milk or water to the conventional recipe to get a pouring consistency.

Amount of time (cooking time) depends on the quantity of food to be cooked. If you increase the quantity of food in the given recipes, time needed for cooking will increase & for lesser amount of food time taken will be less.

SNACKS

Potato based Pizza

Picture on page 9

Serves 4

9" ROUND DISH, 1" HIGH

PIZZA BASE

100 gms maida (1 cup packed)
2 tbsp/30 gms butter
1 medium/100 gms potato
½ tsp baking powder
½ tsp salt

PIZZA SAUCE

4 tbsp ready made tomato puree
½ tsp garam masala, ½ tsp dhania powder
½ tsp oregano or ¼ tsp ajwain - powdered
½ tsp salt, 1 tsp sugar
½ tsp chilli powder

TOPPING
50 gms cheese
½ medium onion - thinly sliced
½ medium capsicum - thinly sliced

1. Put the potato in a polythene bag and micro high 2½ minutes. Mash the cooked potato to a smooth paste. Keep aside to cool.
2. Rub butter into the flour till it resembles bread crumbs.
3. Add mashed potato, baking powder and salt.
4. Knead to a dough using a few tbsp cold water.
5. To prepare the sauce, mix all the ingredients with the tomato puree. Keep aside.
6. Roll out pizza dough and spread out in the dish.
7. Spread sauce on the pizza, leaving ¼" space all around. **Micro high uncovered 6 minutes.**
8. Mix a little salt to onion and capsicum and sprinkle on the pizza. Grate cheese on it. **Micro high uncovered 1 minute.**
9. Let it stand for 2-3 minutes before slicing.

Paneer Tikka

Serves 4-5

400 gms paneer - cut into 1" pieces (¾" thick)
1 tsp garlic paste or 8-10 flakes garlic - crushed
1½ tsp ginger paste or 1½" piece ginger - crushed to a paste
½ tsp kala namak (rock salt)
2 tsp amchoor powder
1 tsp garam masala powder
1 cup curd - hung for 20 minutes to get 6-8 tbsp thick curd
1-½ tsp red chilli powder
¾ -1 tsp salt
2 pinches haldi
2 medium onions - cut into 4 pieces & leaves separated
2 capsicums - each cut into 8 large pieces

1. Cut paneer into flat 1" pieces.
2. Quarter onions and separate leaves.
3. Cut each capsicum into 4-6 large pieces.
4. Mix curd, ginger and garlic paste, kala namak, amchoor, garam masala, red chilli powder, salt and a little haldi to give colour.
5. Add paneer, onion and capsicum to curd paste and let it marinate for 1-2 hours or till serving time.
6. At serving time, place paneer pieces on a plate in a single layer.
7. Micro high uncovered 2 minutes. Turn over the paneer pieces and again **micro high uncovered 2 minutes.**
8. In another plate take onion and capsicum pieces. Arrange in a single layer. **Micro high 2 minutes**.
9. Arrange paneer, capsicum and onion alternately on the serving dish. Serve hot.

Note : If you have the convection mode in the oven, preheat oven to 180°C. Put marinated tikkas on the grill rack and cook for 20 minutes at 180°C. Pour some oil with a spoon on the tikkas to baste them & again cook for 7-8 minutes till crisp on the outside.

Khandavi

Picture on page 19

Very simple to prepare!

Makes 8 rolls

½ cup gram flour (besan)
¾ cup curd
¾ cup water
½ tsp salt, ¼ tsp haldi
pinch of hing (asafoetida)
½" piece ginger - crushed to a paste
1 green chilli - crushed to a paste

TEMPERING (BAGHAR)

1½ tbsp oil
½ tsp rai (mustard seeds) - crushed
1 green chilli - chopped fine (optional)

Khandavi : page 18

few coriander leaves - chopped
a little freshly grated coconut

1. Mix besan, curd and water well with a beater so that no lumps remain.
2. Pour into a dish and **micro uncovered 80% power for 4 minutes**.
3. Add haldi, salt, ginger chilli paste and hing.
4. Stir well and **micro high 3 minutes** or till mixture is thick.
5. Remove from microwave.
6. Mix well & spread quickly, thinly on a plastic sheet. Let it cool for 5-7 minutes. Cut into thin strips (1" broad) & make rolls.
7. For the baghar, **micro high oil uncovered 2 minutes.**
8. Add rai and green chilli. **Micro high uncovered 2 minutes.**
9. Add coriander leaves and coconut. Mix and pour over the prepared khandavi.

Rasmise Aloo Matar : page 38
Sauted Mushrooms : page 64

Delightful Paneer with Grapes

Picture on page 66

Cinnamon flavoured snack served with drinks.

3"-4" (SMALL) ROUND BOWL

Serves 4

100 gms paneer - cut into ¾" cubes
15-20 grapes - washed well
2 tsp oil
a few plastic cocktail forks or wooden tooth picks

MASALA

1 stick dalchini (cinnamon)
3-4 laung (cloves)
½ tsp ajwain (carom seeds)
4-5 chhoti illaichi (green cardamoms)

1. Crush or grind all the ingredients of the masala together to a coarse powder on a chakla-belan or a small spice grinder. Keep aside.
2. **Micro high oil in a small bowl for 2 minutes.** Add the powdered masala. Mix well. Add the paneer pieces. Sprinkle a little salt. Mix very well. Keep aside till serving time.
3. **At serving time, micro high paneer for 1 minute.**
4. Insert a hot paneer piece in the tooth pick & then a grape. Serve with cold drinks before meals.

Masala Idli

Delicious idlis can be on the breakfast table in no time.

Makes 5 big idlis

5 SMALL GLASS (MICRO PROOF) KATORIS (BOWLS)
1 tbsp oil
1-2 green chillies
1 cup suji (rawa)
2 tbsp chopped coriander leaves
½ tsp soda-bicarb
1 cup curd
¼ cup grated coconut
½ cup water
¾ tsp salt

1. Chop coriander leaves and green chillies finely.
2. In a dish **micro high uncovered** 1 tbsp oil for **2 minutes.**
3. Add chillies. **Micro high uncovered for 1 minute.**
4. Add suji (rawa). Mix well. **Micro high uncovered for 1 minute.**
5. Add coriander leaves & salt. Mix well. Allow to cool.
6. Add coconut, curd, water & soda-bicarb. **Keep aside for 10 minutes.**
7. Grease small glass katoris or plastic boxes. Pour 2-3 tbsp mixture into each katori.
8. Arrange in a ring in the microwave and **micro high uncovered for 4 minutes.**
9. Let it stand for 5 minutes. Serve hot with coconut chutney.

Note: One idli takes 1 minute for cooking. So cooking time increases as per the number of idlis. If the idlis are made beforehand, remove from moulds and keep in a covered box. Before serving micro high for 1 minute. Idlis should always be served hot.

Ordinary idlis of rice-dal mixture can also be made similarly in a microwave.

Potato Chaat

Tastes good even at breakfast with buttered toasts & coffee.

Serves 4

4 medium sized potatoes
12 pieces of ready-made potato chips (potato wafers) - crushed roughly
4 tbsp chopped fresh coriander (hara dhania)
½ tsp kala namak, ½ tsp bhuna jeera (roasted cumin powder)
¾ tsp salt or to taste, juice of ½ lemon, 2 tsp oil
1-2 green chillies - deseeded & chopped finely

1. Wash potatoes well. Put them in an ordinary polythene bag. Place in the centre of the microwave. **Micro high for 4 minutes.**
2. Peel the potatoes. Cut into small cubes & place in a flat dish. Sprinkle oil on the potatoes and mix well. Add all the ingredients except the potato chips. **Micro high for 1 minute uncovered.** Keep aside.
3. At serving time, break the potato chips a little and mix with the chaat.

Indian Dishes

Mushroom & Capsicum Bhujia

Serves 4

7-8" ROUND, 1-2" HIGH DISH

100 gms (½ packet) fresh mushrooms - cut into 4 pieces
2 capsicums - chopped into ¼" pieces
2 onions - cut into rings & separated
1" piece ginger - cut into match sticks
1 large tomato - chopped
2 tbsp oil
¼ tsp haldi, ¼ tsp amchoor
½ tsp garam masala, ½ tsp red chilli powder
1 tsp dhania powder
1 tsp salt
1 tsp tandoori masala

Navratan Korma: page 42

1. In a dish **micro high oil & onions together for 2 minutes uncovered.**
2. Add haldi, amchoor, garam masala, red chilli powder and dhania powder. Mix well. **Micro high for 1 minute.**
3. Add tomatoes. Mix. Add ginger, mushrooms, capsicums, salt and tandoori masala. Mix very well.
4. **Micro high 8 minutes. Stir once in-between.** Serve.

Spinach & Carrot Rice : page 58

Zayekedar Arbi

Serves 3-4

8" ROUND, 1-2" HIGH DISH

10 medium sized pieces of arbi (400 gm) - peeled & halved lengthways
1" piece ginger - grated finely
4-5 flakes garlic - chopped & crushed
1-2 green chillies - chopped very finely
¾ tsp salt
juice of ½ lemon
1 tsp ajwain - crushed roughly

MASALA

6 tbsp thick curd
1 tsp besan (gram flour)
1 tbsp fresh coriander chopped
1 tbsp (poodina) mint leaves - chopped

2 tsp oil
½ tsp salt, ½ tsp red chilli pd., ½ tsp garam masala, ½ tsp amchoor

1. Choose even sized arbi and it should not be too thick. Peel, slit into half length ways. If the arbi is thick, cut lengthways into 3 pieces. Rub 2 tsp salt on it nicely and keep aside for 10 minutes or more. Wash well. Strain. Wipe dry.
2. Place arbi in a flat dish. Sprinkle all the ingredients given under the arbi on it. Rub them well over the arbi.
3. **Micro high 2 minutes uncovered.** Turn pieces over with tongs or spoon. **Again micro high 2 minutes uncovered.**
4. Beat curd with a spoon in a small bowl. Add all the other ingredients and mix well.
5. Sprinkle the dahi mix on the arbi and mix well. **Micro high covered for 6 minutes.**
6. Let stand for 2 minutes. Serve sprinkled with a little lemon juice.

Corn Korma

Serves 6-7

8" ROUND, 2½"-3" DEEP DISH WITH COVER

3 tbsp oil
2 medium onions - chopped finely
3-4 moti illaichi (black cardamoms)
1 tsp red chilli powder, salt to taste, ¼ tsp sugar
¼ tsp haldi (turmeric) powder
1 cup frozen or tinned corn
2 green chillies - deseeded & chopped

GRIND TO A PASTE

1 cup curd, 1 tomato
1 small piece coconut - grated (¼ cup)
2 tsp khus-khus (poppy seeds)
7-8 cashewnuts or 2 tsp magaz
2-3 green chillies

GARNISHING
a few coriander leaves - chopped finely

1. Grind all the ingredients of the masala paste together to a fine paste.
2. In the dish take oil. Add slightly opened cardamoms. **Micro high 2 minutes uncovered.**
3. Add sugar, red chilli powder, salt and haldi powder. Mix well. Add onions. **Micro high 3 minutes.**
4. Add curd paste. Mix well. **Micro high 5 minutes. Stir once in between.**
5. Add corn. Add green chillies and garam masala. Mix well. **Micro high covered 2 minutes.**
6. Let stand for 3-4 minutes.
7. Sprinkle chopped coriander leaves and serve hot.

Saunf ke Karele

Picture on page 65

Serves 4-5

7-8 " ROUND, 1-2" HIGH DISH (FLAT DISH)

½ kg karelas (bitter gourd) - peeled, slit, seeds removed & rubbed with salt & kept aside for 2-3 hours
4 onions - chopped
½" piece ginger - chopped finely
2 green chillies - chopped finely
3 tbsp oil
2 tsp moti saunf (big aniseeds)

DRY MASALA

¼ tsp haldi, ½ tsp salt
1 tsp amchoor (dried mango powder)
½ tsp red chilli powder, ½ tsp garam masala

1. Peel karelas. Give a cut in the centre. Carefully remove all the seeds. Rub salt inside and over the karelas. Keep aside for 2-3 hours or more. You could do this part of the work in the morning and put away the karelas in the fridge, if they have to be prepared for dinner.
2. Wash kerelas well to remove bitterness. **Micro high uncovered 8 minutes on a plate or a flat dish.**
3. In a flat dish, **micro high oil for 3 minutes.**
4. Add saunf. Mix well. Add onions, ginger and green chillies. Sprinkle all the ingredients given under dry masala. Mix very well. **Micro high 7 minutes. Stir once in between.**
5. Fill the stuffing in the karelas. Close the sides with the help of a wooden tooth pick. Arrange in the same dish, side by side. Sprinkle 1 tbsp oil over the karelas.
6. **Cover and micro high 4 minutes.** Serve.

Rasmise Aloo Matar

Picture on page 20

Serves 4-5

6"-7" ROUND, 4"-5" DEEP DISH

1 cup shelled peas (matar)
1 potato - cut into ½" cubes (small even cubes)
2 medium onions - minced (chopped very finely)
2-3 flakes garlic - chopped finely
½ " piece ginger - chopped finely
3 tbsp oil
¼ tsp haldi
½-1 tsp red chilli powder
2 tsp dhania powder
½ tsp garam masala powder
2 large tomatoes - ground to a puree
1 tsp salt
1 tbsp coriander leaves - chopped

1. In a deep dish, **micro high uncovered oil, onion, ginger & garlic for 4 minutes.**
2. Add haldi powder, dhania powder, garam masala powder, red chilli powder. Mix well.
3. Add tomato puree. Mix well. **Micro high uncovered 6 minutes. Stir once in between.**
4. Add shelled peas, potatoes and 1 cup water. Mix well.
5. **Micro high covered 5-7 minutes or till potatoes become soft.**
6. Add salt and coriander leaves.
7. **Micro high 1 minute.**
8. Let stand 2-3 minutes. Serve hot.

Kati Bhindi

Picture on back cover

Serves 3-4

8"-9" ROUND, 1- 2" HIGH DISH

300 gms bhindi (lady fingers) - cut into ¼" pieces (small pieces)
3 tbsp oil
1 medium onion - sliced finely
½ tsp dhania powder, ½ tsp garam masala powder
½ tsp haldi (turmeric) powder, ½ tsp red chilli powder
¾ tsp salt, ½ tsp amchoor (dried mango powder), 2-3 green chillies

1. **Micro high oil uncovered in a flat dish for 3 minutes.**
2. Add haldi, dhania powder, red chilli and garam masala. Mix well. Add onion and bhindi. Mix well. **Micro high uncovered 7 minutes.**
3. Sprinkle 1 tsp salt and amchoor powder over it. Mix very well. Add whole green chillies. Mix. **Micro high uncovered 2 minutes.**
4. **Cover and Micro high for 2 minutes.** Let it stand for 2-3 minutes and then serve.

Kadhai Paneer

Picture on page 83

Serves 4

6" ROUND, 3" DEEP DISH WITH COVER

200 gms paneer - cut in 1" cubes, 1 capsicum - cut into thin long strips
2 tbsp oil, 5-6 flakes garlic - crushed
4 tbsp ready made tomato puree
1 tsp kasoori methi (dry fenugreek leaves)
1 tsp salt, ½ tsp sugar, ¾ tsp red chilli powder (to taste)
1 tsp dhania powder, ½ tsp garam masala

1. In a dish add oil and garlic. **Micro high uncovered 2 minutes.**
2. Add tomato puree and kasoori methi. Add salt, sugar, red chilli pd, dhania and garam masala. Mix well. Add capsicum. Mix. **Micro high uncovered for 3 minutes.**
3. Add paneer. Mix well. Keep aside. **At serving time, Micro high covered for 2 minutes.** Serve hot.

Navratan Korma

Picture on page 29

Serves 5-6

6"-7" ROUND, 4-5" DEEP DISH

¼ of a small cauliflower (8 small flowerets of ½" size)
1 carrot - cut into slightly thick round slices
½ cup shelled peas
10 french beans - cut into ½" pieces
1 capsicum - cut into ½" cubes
100 gm paneer - cut into ½" cubes
2 onions
½" piece ginger
3-4 flakes garlic
3 tomatoes pureed in the mixer (or 1 cup tomato puree)
1 tsp dhania powder, ¾ tsp jeera - crushed to a powder
½ tsp garam masala powder, 1 tsp red chilli powder

2 tbsp ghee or oil
50 gms khoya - grated
1½ tsp salt
chopped coriander leaves, 2 laung (cloves) - crushed to a powder

1. Cut all the vegetables into ½" pieces.
2. Grind together onion, ginger and garlic.
3. Cut tomatoes into small pieces and blend well in the mixer.
4. Put onion paste in the dish. Sprinkle oil on it. Mix well. **Micro high 5 minutes uncovered.**
5. Add tomato puree, all vegetables (except paneer), jeera powder, garam masala powder, dhania powder & red chilli powder. Mix well.
6. **Micro high covered 8 minutes. Stir once in between.**
7. Add grated khoya, paneer and salt. Mix well.
8. **Micro high covered 4 minutes. Stir once in between.**
9. Let stand 2 minutes.
10. Add laung and chopped coriander leaves. Sprinkle grated khoya at serving time.

Khoya Matar

Picture on cover

An excellent preparation!

Serves 3-4

6"-7" ROUND DISH, 2" HIGH WITH COVER

100 gms khoya - grated
1 cup matar (shelled peas)
3 tbsp oil or 2 tbsp desi ghee
1 medium sized onion
1-2 green chillies
½" piece ginger
3 tbsp ready made tomato puree
¼ - ½ tsp red chili powder
½ tsp jeera (cumin) powder
½ tsp garam masala powder
a few cashewnuts - optional
¾ tsp salt

1. In a dish, **micro high uncovered oil for 2 minutes.**
2. Grind together onion, green chillies and ginger. Add onion paste to oil. Mix well.
3. **Micro high uncovered for 4 minutes.**
4. Add tomato puree, garam masala, red chilli powder, jeera powder, peas and 3-4 tbsp water. Mix well.
5. **Micro high uncovered for 3 minutes.**
6. Add salt, grated khoya, 6-7 tbsp water and cashewnuts. Mix gently so as not to mash the khoya.
7. **Micro high covered for 2 minutes.**
8. Serve hot.

Bharvaan Baingan

Serves 4-5

7" - 8" ROUND DISH, 1-2 " HIGH WITH COVER
250 gm small baingans, 2 tbsp oil
4-5 thick green chillies, 1¼ tsp salt, ½ tsp red chilli powder
½ tsp garam masala, 2 tsp dhania powder
½ tsp amchoor, ½ tsp haldi
½ tsp sugar, juice of ½ lemon (1 tbsp)

1. Wash, slit brinjals, making cross cuts. Slit green chillies. Deseed them.
2. Mix salt, sugar, chilli powder, garam masala, amchoor, dhania powder & haldi together. Add a little lemon juice to make a wet paste.
3. Fill the paste in the baingans and green chillies.
4. Arrange in a dish. Pour oil on them. **Micro high covered for 6 minutes.** Serve hot.

Corn & Cheese in Mustard Sauce: page 72

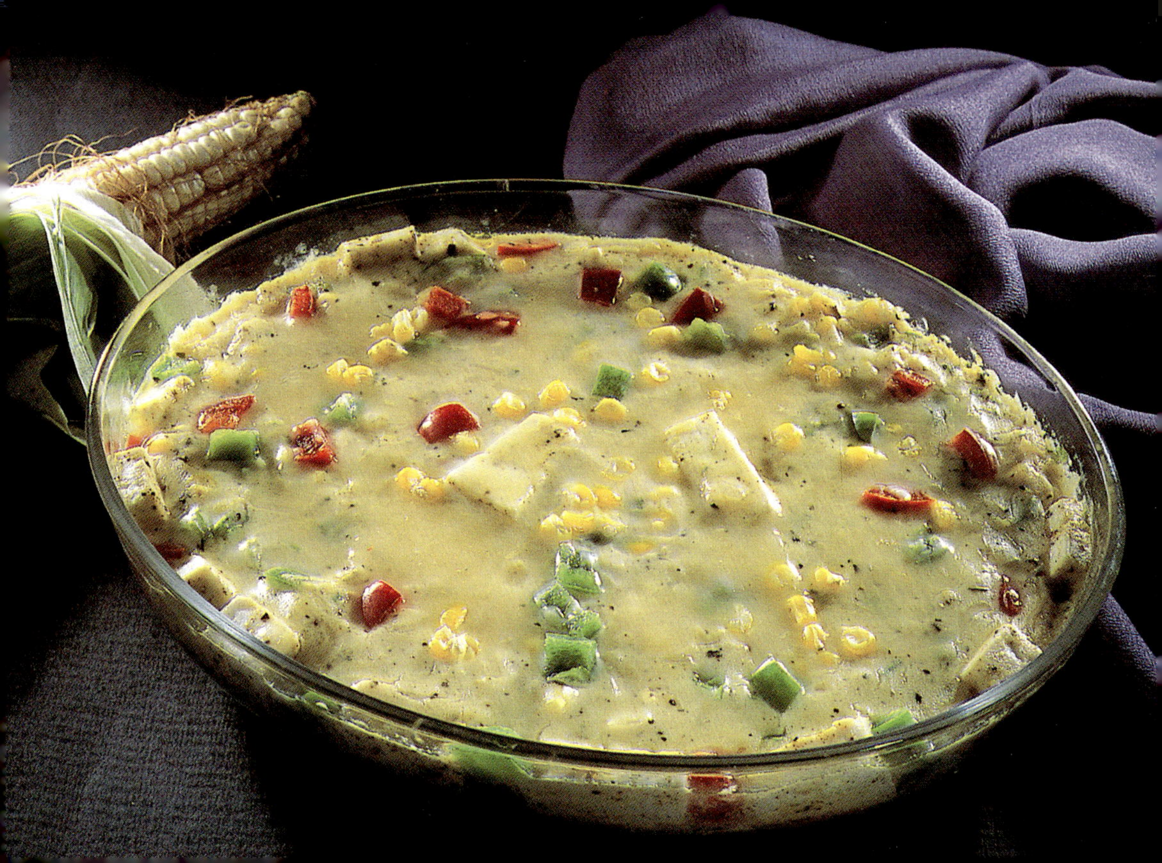

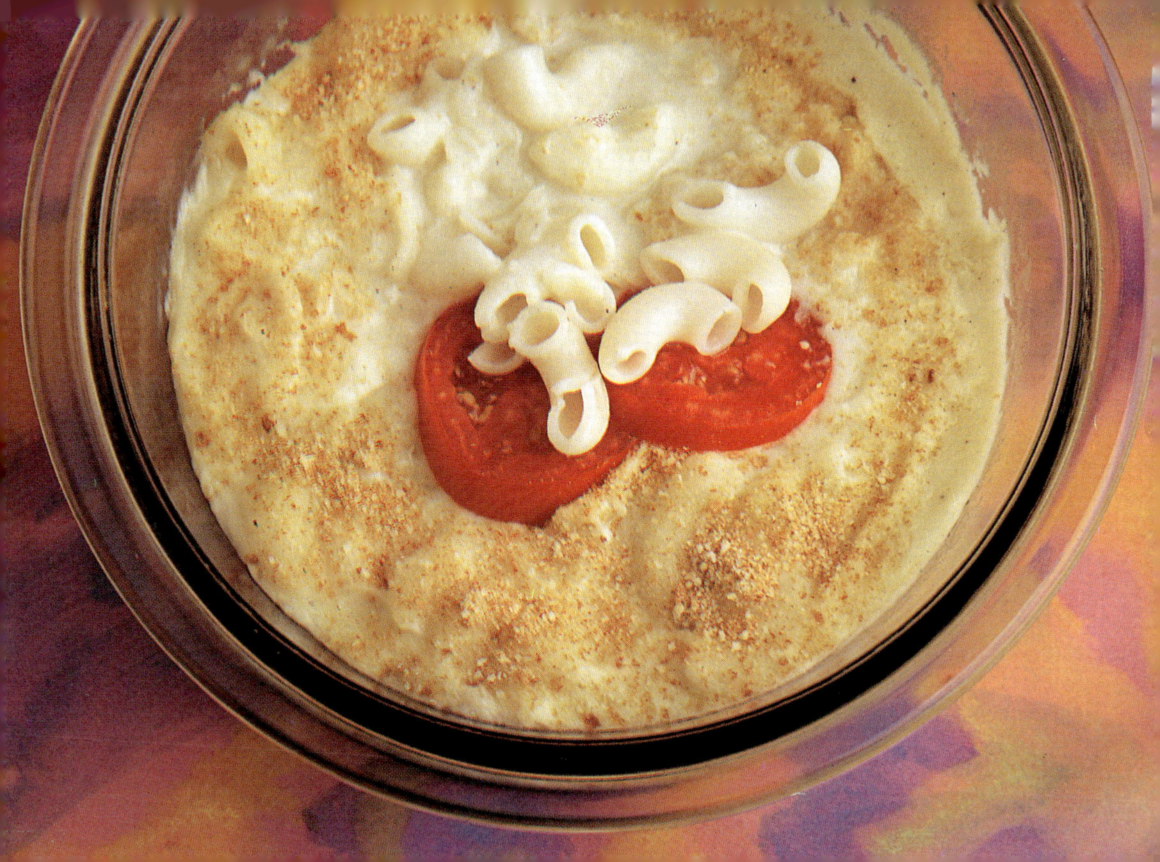

Paneer Hara Pyaz

Picture on inside front cover

Serves 4-5

200 gm paneer- cut into 1" cubes
150 gm hare pyaaz (spring onions), 1 green chilli - deseeded & chopped
3 tbsp oil, 6-8 flakes garlic - crushed, ¼ tsp haldi, 2 tsp dhania powder
¾ cup tomato puree (readymade)
1 tbsp tomato ketchup, 3 laung (cloves) - crushed, ½ tsp red chilli powder
½ tsp garam masala, ½ tsp salt, 4 tbsp cream or well beaten thin malai

1. Cut white of spring onions into rings, greens into ½" diagonal pieces.
2. Put oil, garlic, white of onion, haldi and dhania powder in a micro proof dish. **Micro high for 5 minutes.**
3. Add tomato puree, tomato ketchup, laung, red chilli powder, garam masala and salt. Mix well. **Micro high for 5 minutes.**
4. Add ½ cup water. Mix paneer, green chillies, cream and about 1 cup of greens of spring onions. Mix well. **Micro high for 2 minutes.**

Macaroni Cheese : page 70

Paneer Makhani

Serves 4-5

6-8 " ROUND DISH, 5- 6" DEEP

300 gms paneer - cut into cubes
4 large (400 gm) tomatoes - chopped roughly
½" piece ginger - chopped
2 tbsp ghee
½ tsp garam masala
½ tsp chilli powder
2 chhoti illaichi (green cardamom) - powdered
2 tbsp cashewnuts or magaz - soaked in ¼ cup water & ground to a paste
1 tsp kasoori methi (dried fenugreek leaves)
1 tsp sugar
1½ tsp salt or to taste
3-4 tbsp cream or fresh malai

1. **Micro high tomatoes and ginger in a deep dish with ¼ cup water for 5 minutes.**
2. Blend cooked tomatoes and ginger to a puree in a mixi.
3. Micro high ghee for 2 minutes. Add illaichi powder. Mix. Add salt, sugar, red chilli powder and garam masala. Mix. Add the prepared tomato puree. **Micro high uncovered 3 minutes.**
4. Add cashewnut or magaz paste and methi. Mix well.
5. **Micro high 2 minutes.**
6. Add paneer and cream (beaten well if using malai). **Micro covered 3-4 minutes.**
7. Sprinkle little kasoori methi on top and serve hot.

Makhani Korma

Serves 4-5

8"-9" ROUND DISH, 4-5" DEEP

2 medium carrots - cut into ½" pieces
1 large potato or turnip - chopped (1½ cups) *(turnip tastes very good)*
2 cups small florets of cauliflower
10-12 french beans - cut into ½" pieces
¼ cup milk
½ cup cream or malai (opt)
½ tsp garam masala powder
¼ tsp pepper
1 tsp salt
3-4 chhoti illaichi (green cardamom) - powdered
1 tbsp chopped coriander
3-4 almonds - cut into thin long pieces for garnishing

MAKHANI SAUCE

2 tsp ghee or oil
4 large (400 gm) tomatoes
2" piece ginger
1 tsp salt, 1 tsp red chilli powder
¾ tsp garam masala powder, ¾ tsp jeera (cumin seeds) - powdered
½ cup cream mixed with ½ cup milk

1. Cut all the vegetables into ½" pieces.
2. Put vegetables in a deep dish. Add ¼ cup milk. **Cover micro high 10 minutes.** Transfer the vegetables to another dish.
3. Prepare makhani sauce by blending the tomatoes to a puree together with all the ingredients given under the sauce, except cream.
4. **Micro high covered 10 minutes in the emptied dish.** Add cream. Mix well. Keep makhani sauce aside.
5. Add garam masala, pepper, salt, cardamom powder & coriander to the cooked makhani sauce. Add vegetables also. **Micro high 4 minutes.** Garnish with almonds. Serve hot.

Mixed Masala Subzi

Picture on page 65

Serves 4

8-9" ROUND, 2" HIGH DISH.

4 small carrots - cut into small even sized pieces
100 gm (25-30) french beans - threaded & cut into ¼" pieces
2 onions - chopped
2 tomatoes - chopped
½ tsp haldi
½ tsp red chilli powder
½ tsp garam masala
1 tsp dhania powder
1 tsp salt or to taste
2 laung (cloves) - crushed
50 gms khoya - grated (optional)

1. Wash chopped beans and carrots. Transfer to a flat micro proof dish. **Cover and micro high for 5 minutes** without adding any water or till vegetables turn soft. Remove from dish.
2. **Micro high 2 tbsp oil in the same dish for 2 minutes.**
3. Add haldi, red chilli, garam masala, dhania and salt. Mix well. **Add onions and micro high for 4 minutes.**
4. Add the cooked beans and carrots. Mix in the tomatoes. **Cover and micro high for 6-7 minutes.**
5. Remove from microwave. Sprinkle 2 tbsp grated khoya and keep aside.
6. At serving time, **micro high for 2 minutes.** Serve.

Stir fried Baby Corns

Serves 3-4

200 gm baby corns
1 capsicum - cut into finger shaped pieces
1 large onion - sliced, 1 tsp finely chopped ginger
1 small tomato - cut into long pieces
2 chhoti illaichi (green cardamom) - crushed to a rough powder
¼ tsp ajwain - crushed to a rough powder
¼ tsp haldi
¼ tsp garam masala
¼ tsp red chilli powder
½ - 3/4 tsp salt
2 tbsp oil

1. Cut each baby corn into 2 pieces lengthways.
2. **Micro high oil, onions, ginger and baby corn together for 3 minutes.**
3. Add haldi, red chilli powder, garam masala and salt. Mix well.
4. Add capsicum strips, tomato pieces, chhoti illaichi and ajwain. **Micro high 3 minutes.**
5. Let stand for 2 minutes. Serve hot.

Spinach & Carrot Rice

Picture on page 30

Serves 4

9-10" ROUND, 2-3" HIGH DISH

150 gm spinach (palak) - leaves cut into thin strips (2 cups)
2 carrots - grated
1 cup basmati rice - soaked for 1 hour
2 tbsp desi ghee or oil
1 tsp saunf
1 onion - sliced finely
2 moti illaichi (brown cardamoms)
1 stick dalchini (cinnamon)
2 laung (cloves)
1½ tsp salt
¼ tsp red chilli powder
2 green chillies

1. Soak rice for 1 hour.
2. Put ghee in a big, flat dish. Add saunf. Mix well. Add moti illaichi, dalchini and laung. Mix well with the ghee. Add onions. **Micro high uncovered all together for 3 minutes.**
3. Add washed spinach and grated carrots. **Micro high uncovered for 2 minutes.**
4. Drain the water from the rice & add the soaked rice to the spinach.
5. Add the salt & red chilli powder. Add 2 cups water. Mix very well.
6. **Micro high covered 12 minutes. Stir once in-between after 5 minutes with a fork.**
7. Let stand for 2 minutes. Fluff it up with a fork to separate the grains. Serve hot.

Matar waale Chaawal

Serves 4

9-10" ROUND, 2-3 " HIGH DISH
1 cup basmati rice - soaked for 1 hour
1 cup shelled peas
½" piece ginger - grated
1 large onion- sliced finely
1½ tsp salt
¼ tsp red chilli powder
¼ tsp garam masala
2-3 laung (cloves)
2 green chillies
2 tbsp chopped coriander
1 firm tomato - cut into strips & pulp removed
3 tbsp oil

1. **Micro high oil in a large dish for 2 minutes.**
2. Add peas, onions, ginger, salt, chilli powder, garam masala & laung. **Micro high for 3 minutes.**
3. Drain the rice and add to it. Add 2 cups water, whole green chillies, coriander leaves and tomato strips. Mix well.
4. **Micro high covered 11 minutes. Stir once after 5 minutes.**
5. Let stand for 2 minutes. Fluff it up with a fork to separate the grains. Serve hot.

Sukhi Dhuli Urad Dal

Picture on page 10

Serves 4

7-8" ROUND, 4-5" DEEP DISH WITH A WELL FITTING LID

1 cup dhuli urad dal (split black beans) - soaked for 1 hour
1 onion - sliced
1" piece ginger - grated
3 tbsp oil
1¼ tsp salt, ½ tsp haldi
½ tsp red chilli powder, ¼ tsp amchoor, ¼ tsp dhania powder

1. Clean and wash dal. Soak in water for 1 hour.
2. Keep onion & ginger in a dish. Sprinkle oil on it. Mix. Add salt, haldi, chilli pd, amchoor & dhania pd. **Micro high uncovered 5 minutes.**
3. Drain the dal and add to the onions. Add 2 cups water. Mix well. **Micro high covered 20 minutes.** Stir once after 8 minutes in-between. Let stand 3 minutes. Sprinkle chopped coriander & mix gently with a fork.

Continental Dishes

Sauted Mushrooms

Picture on page 20

Serves 3-4

8"-9" ROUND, 1"- 2 " HIGH DISH
200 gm mushrooms - sliced thickly
3 tbsp oil
1 large onion - sliced
4 flakes garlic - minced or crushed
½ tsp jeera (cumin seeds) - crushed roughly to a powder
1 tsp salt
½ tsp pepper
3 tbsp milk
1 tsp cornflour
2 tbsp chopped coriander leaves

Saunf ke Karele : page 36
Mixed Masala Subzi : page 54

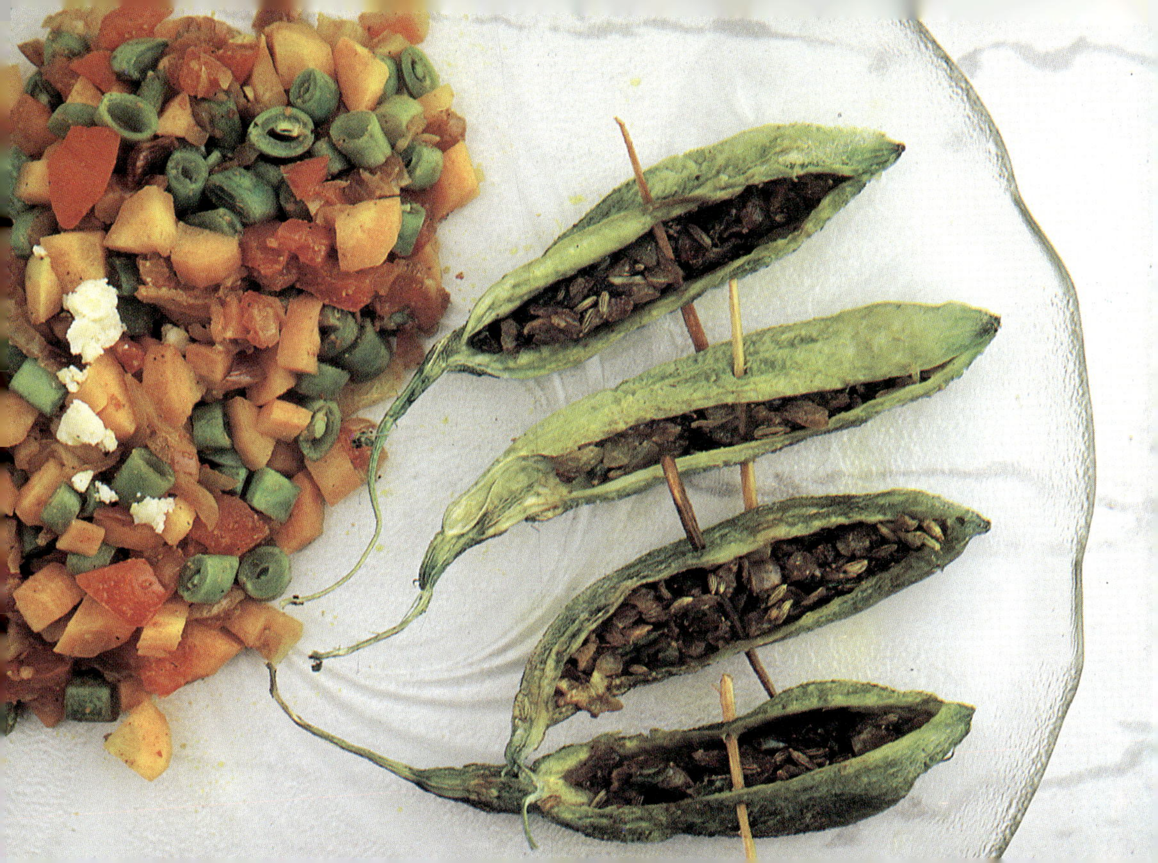

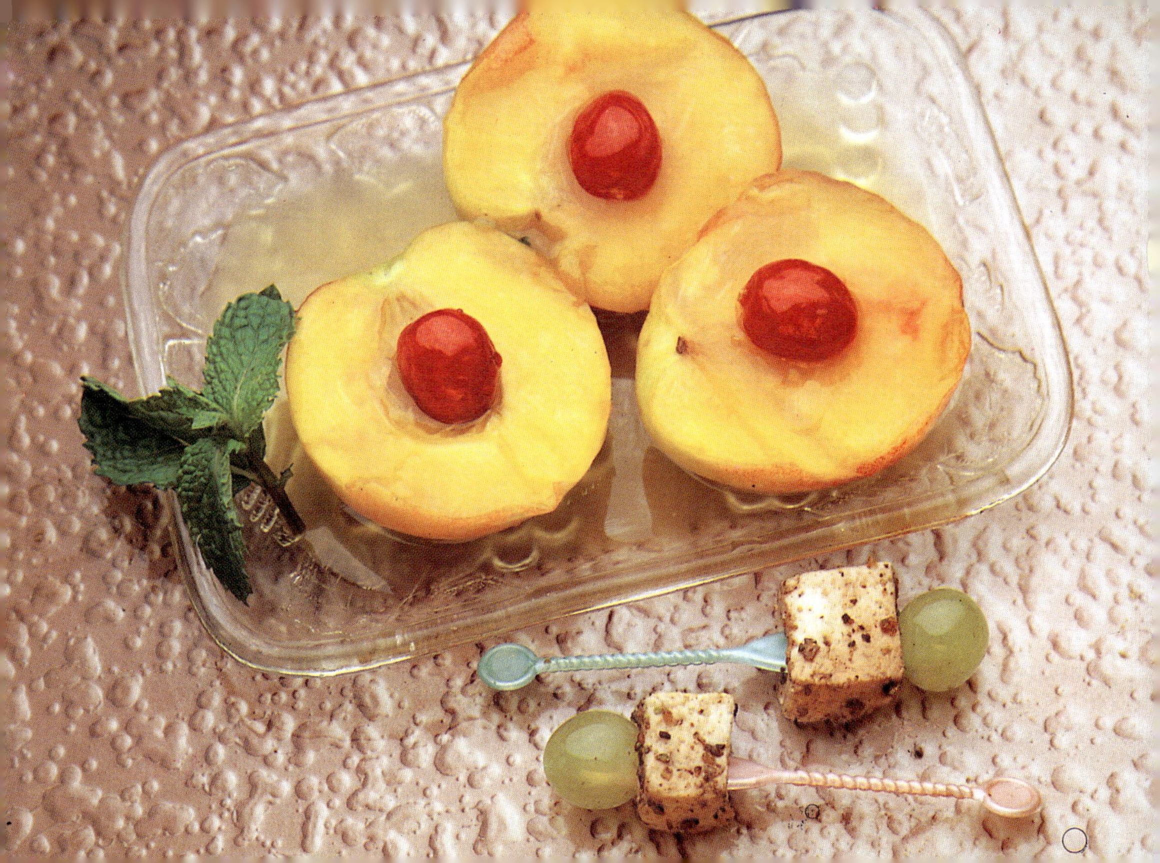

1. **Micro high oil in the dish uncovered for 2 minutes.**
2. Add sliced onion, garlic, cumin powder and **micro high uncovered for 3 minutes.**
3. Mix in mushroom and **micro high covered for 5 minutes.**
4. Mix milk & cornflour.
5. Add to the mushrooms and mix well. Sprinkle salt and pepper and mix well.
6. **Micro high covered 1 minute.**
7. Sprinkle chopped coriander leaves and serve hot.

Stewed Peaches : page 76
Delightful Paneer with Grapes : page 22

Stuffed Tomatoes

Serves 5-6

5 large or 6 medium sized tomatoes
1 cup cottage cheese (paneer) - mashed roughly
½ cup onion - chopped fine
½ cup capsicum - chopped fine
½ cup boiled green peas
2 tbsp tomato ketchup
2 tbsp chilli sauce
¾ tsp salt
½ tsp garam masala
1 tsp amchoor (dried mango powder) powder
coriander leaves

1. Cut tomatoes into 2 halves. Remove pulp & keep inverted for 3-4 minutes.
2. Mix all other ingredients well.
3. Spoon filling into tomato halves and place in a ring on a plate in the microwave.
4. **Micro high uncovered 2-3 minutes or until tomatoes are tender.**
5. **If combination present instead of step 4 keep tomatoes in combination 5 minutes.**
6. Allow to stand 2 minutes. Serve hot garnished with coriander leaves.

Note: Lightly score the tomato skin so as to prevent the tomatoes from splitting.

Variation:

Stuffed capsicums can be made in the same way. Filling of your choice can be used.

Macaroni Cheese

Picture on page 48

Serves 3-4

5-6" ROUND DISH, 4-5 " DEEP

1 cup uncooked macaroni (small)
2 tbsp butter
1 onion or 2 spring onions - chopped along with green parts
2½ tbsp flour (maida)
1¾ cups milk
¾ tsp salt
½ tsp pepper
¼ tsp mustard powder
25 gm cheese (1 cube) - grated
1 tbsp bread crumbs
some tomato slices & chopped coriander leaves

1. Micro high 1½ cups of water with 1 tsp oil in a medium sized deep dish uncovered for 3 minutes.
2. Add macaroni. **Micro high uncovered 5 minutes.**
3. Let stand in hot water 4-5 minutes. Drain and wash well with cold water.
4. In a clean dish, **micro high butter 1 minute.**
5. Add spring onions and **micro high covered 2 minutes.**
6. Add flour. Mix well and **micro high uncovered 30 seconds.**
7. Add milk. Stir well, so that no lumps are formed.
8. Add salt, pepper and **micro high uncovered 3 minutes stirring after every minute to avoid lump formation. Microwave for 1-2 minutes more** if the sauce does not turn thick.
9. Add mustard powder, boiled macaroni, grated cheese. Mix well.
10. Sprinkle bread crumbs on top. Arrange 2-3 tomato slices and sprinkle a little chopped coriander. **Micro high uncovered 2 minutes** or if you have a grill mode **grill the dish for 15 minutes**. Serve.

Corn & Cheese in Mustard Sauce

Picture on page 47

Serves 4

7-8" ROUND DISH, 2" HIGH

200 gm cottage cheese (paneer) - cut into thin, 1" pieces
¼ cup chopped green capsicum, ¼ cup chopped red capsicum
¾ cup tinned corn kernels, 6 tbsp grated mozzarella cheese

MARINADE

1 tbsp mustard paste, 1 tsp lemon juice
¼ tsp freshly ground (saboot kali mirch) peppercorns, ½ tsp salt

MUSTARD SAUCE

2 tbsp butter
1 small onion - finely chopped, 2 tbsp maida (plain flour)
2 cups milk
½ tsp dried basil or 2 tbsp fresh basil leaves
¾ tsp salt, 1 tsp mustard paste, ½ tsp pepper

1. Sprinkle all ingredients of the marinade on paneer and mix well.
2. For the sauce, **micro high butter for 1 minute**.
3. Add onions and **micro high covered for 2 minutes**.
4. Add flour. Mix well and **micro high uncovered for 30 seconds**.
5. Add capsicum and corn. Mix well.
6. Add milk. Stir well so that there are no lumps.
7. Add salt, pepper, mustard, basil and mix well.
8. **Micro high uncovered for 3 minutes, stirring after every 1 minute** to avoid lump formation. Micro high for 1-2 minutes more if the sauce does not turn thick.
9. Arrange marinated paneer in a greased dish.
10. Pour the sauce over it.
11. Grate cheese on it.
12. Sprinkle some chopped red and green capsicum and 1-2 tbsp tinned corn on it. **Micro high 2-3 minutes** till cheese melts or **grill in the oven for 15 minutes**. Serve hot.

Mushroom Fondue

A great success! Can be spread on toasted bread & served as a cocktail snack.

Serves 3-4

.6" ROUND, 2½ " HIGH DISH

200 gms mushrooms - sliced, 1 cup water
2 tbsp oil
1 medium onion - sliced (1 cup)
2 tbsp flour (maida)
½ tsp salt, ½ tsp pepper

1. **Micro high covered 1 cup water & sliced mushrooms for 5 minutes.**
2. In a casserole **micro high oil uncovered for 1 minute.** Add sliced onion. **Micro high uncovered 2 minutes.**
3. Add flour. Mix well. **Micro high uncovered 2 minutes.**
4. Add salt, pepper, mushrooms along with the water in which they are cooked. Mix well. **Micro high uncovered 2 minutes.** Serve hot.

Desserts

Stewed Peaches in Sauce

Picture on page 66

Serves 4

6-7 " ROUND, 1-1½" HIGH DISH
4 big (ripe & firm) peaches (aadus)
6 tbsp sugar
8-10 tbsp water

SAUCE
1 tbsp vanilla custard powder dissolved in ¼ cup water

DECORATION
a few grapes
a few almonds - split into 2 halves

1. Wash peaches well. Divide into two halves by running a knife all around at the centre. Pull the two parts apart to divide into two equal halves. Remove the seed carefully.
2. Place them in a flat dish. Sprinkle sugar with a tbsp on all the peaches.
3. Pour a tbsp of water on each piece.
4. **Micro high 4 minutes or till the peaches turn very soft**, depending upon the ripeness of the fruit.
5. Remove the stewed peaches in a clean serving dish, leaving behind the sugar syrup. Arrange properly and keep aside.
6. Dissolve custard powder in ¼ cup water and add to the sugar syrup.
7. **Micro high the sugar syrup for 1 minute, stirring once after 80 seconds** or when it starts to boil, to prevent lumps from forming.
8. Pour the ready sauce over the arranged peaches in the dish. Decorate the peaches by placing a fresh cherry or a grape in the centre of each piece and a piece of almond with it.

Benarasi Kheer

Serves 6-8

10" ROUND, 5" DEEP DISH
1 kg (6 cups) milk
½ cup rice
½ tin milkmaid
10-15 almonds - blanched & chopped
10-15 raisins - soaked in water & squeezed
2-3 chhoti illaichi (green cardamom) - powdered
1 tsp saffron (kesar) - optional

1. **Micro high milk & rice together uncovered for 20 minutes. Stir once after 8-10 minutes.**
2. Add milkmaid & kesar. Mix well.
3. **Micro high uncovered 10 minutes.** Stir in between.
4. **Simmer (micro) at 50% power 5 minutes.** Remove from microwave and mash well with a potato masher or a karchhi to break the rice grains.
5. Add almonds & raisins.
6. Cool. Add illaichi powder.
7. Chill & serve.

Note: Kheer becomes thick on cooling. Extra milk may be added to thin it down.

Variations:

Kheer of suji (rawa), vermicilli (seviyan) can also be made similarly.

Phirni

Serves 3-4

7"-8" ROUND, 4-5" DEEP DISH

3½ cups milk
¼ cup rice - soaked for 2-3 hours & ground to a fine paste
7-8 tbsp (level) powdered sugar
1 tsp kewra or rose water - (optional) or a drop of kewra essence
2-3 chhoti iliaichi (green cardamom) - powdered
varak (silver leaf)
5-6 green pistas - sliced into thin long pieces
2 almonds - sliced into thin long pieces

1. Soak rice in a little water for 2-3 hours. Grind in the mixer with a little water to a very fine paste.
2. In a dish mix ground rice and milk.
3. **Micro high uncovered 6 minutes. Stir with a karchhi, after every minute otherwise lumps will form.** Break lumps if any.
4. Add sugar. Mix well. **Micro high uncovered 3 minutes, stirring in-between.**
5. Mix well. Cool. Add rose/kewra water & illaichi powder. Leave to set.
6. Decorate with varak, nuts & illaichi powder. Serve chilled.

Note:
1. Sets very well in earthen ware pots (small kullhar)
2. Must stir after every 1 minute otherwise lumps get formed.
3. Beat well with an electric beater if lumps do appear.

Nutty Mango Sauce

Enjoy it plain or over a scoop of vanilla ice cream.

Serves 5-6

7" ROUND, 3" DEEP DISH
4 tbsp gur (jaggery)
2 tbsp unsalted butter
¼ tsp chhoti illaichi (green cardamom) powder
¼ tsp dalchini (cinnamon) powder
10-12 almonds - sliced
2 tbsp cornflour dissolved in 4-5 tbsp water
2 big ripe mangoes - finely chopped (3 cups)

Kadhai Paneer : page 41

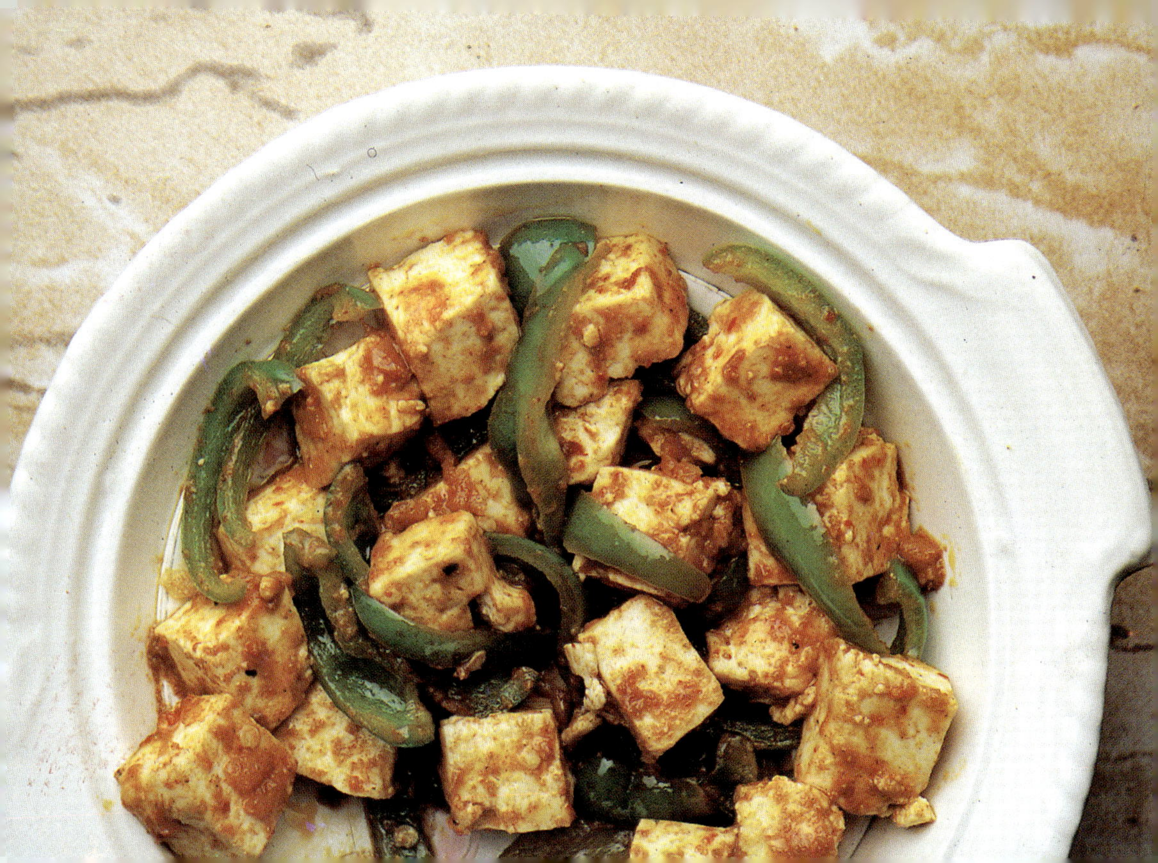

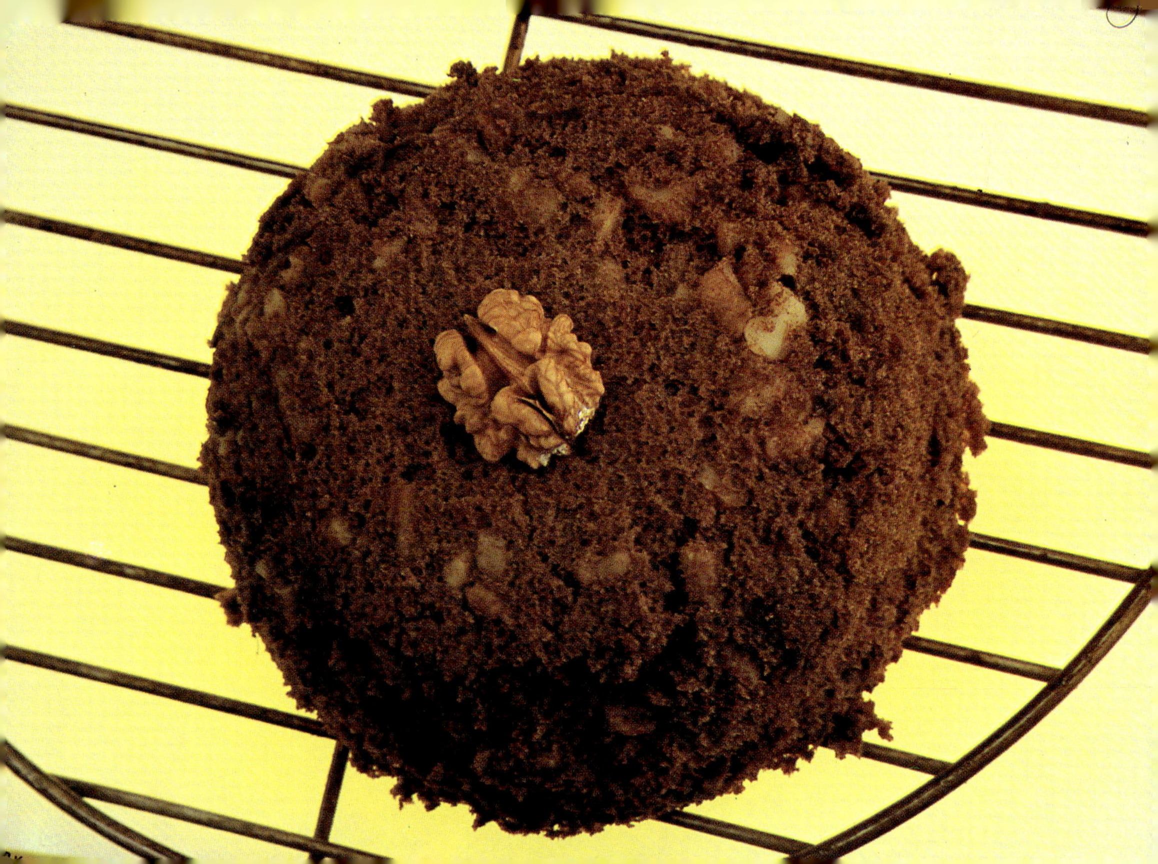

1. Mix ½ cup water, gur & butter. **Micro at 50% power uncovered for 3 minutes. Stir well.**
2. Stir in cornflour dissolved in water, cardamom powder, dalchini powder & almonds. **Micro high uncovered for 2 minutes.**
3. Mix finely chopped mangoes (or you can puree them in the mixer for a smoother sauce).
4. **Micro high uncovered 3 minutes.**
5. Let stand 2-3 minutes.
6. Serve hot or cold, plain or with vanilla ice-cream.

Note: Sauce of other fruits like pear, peaches, strawberry, apples can be made with the above recipe. Adjust gur (jaggery) according to the sweetness of the fruit.

Chocolate Walnut Cake : page 90

Mango Bread Pudding

Serves 5-6

8" ROUND, 3" DEEP DISH

7 slices of bread
1½ tsp baking powder
¼ tsp chhoti illaichi (green cardamom) powder
¼ cup kishmish (raisins)
2 tbsp powdered sugar
100 gms khoya - grated
a few mango slices
a few chopped almonds
3 cups nutty mango sauce (recipe on page 82)

1. Remove sides of bread slices. Soak bread in water. Squeeze and crumble well. Keep aside.
2. Prepare nutty sauce as given on page 82.
3. Mix crumbled bread with the prepared sauce. Add cardamom powder, baking powder, kishmish and grated khoya. Mix well.
4. **Micro high uncovered 5 minutes or till surface feels firm to touch.**
5. Serve warm or cold, according to the season, decorated with mango slices & chopped almonds.

Variation: Puddings of other fruits like apples, peaches, pears, strawberries etc can be made in the same way.

Gajar ka Halwa

Picture on cover

Serves 5-6

10" ROUND, 5" DEEP DISH

½ kg carrots - grated
1½ cups milk
½ - ¾ cup sugar - powdered
½ cup (100 gms) khoya - grated
2-3 tbsp desi ghee
some chopped nuts like almonds, raisins (kishmish) etc.

1. Mix grated carrots and milk.
2. **Micro high uncovered 15 minutes. Mix once after 5 minutes.**
3. Add sugar & khoya. Mix well.
4. **Micro high 10 minutes uncovered.**
5. Add ghee. Mix well. **Micro high 7 minutes**. Mix chopped nuts. Serve hot or cold decorated with nuts.

Tips for Cake Making

- Always use powdered sugar. Ordinary sugar gets burnt. So, grind sugar & keep in a box if you want to microwave cakes.
- Mixture should be a little thinner than soft dropping consistency. Add a little milk to the conventional recipe if you want to microwave the cake.
- Preferably use round dishes & do not cover while cooking.
- Give a little standing time after the microwave switches off. The cake **appears wet and quite undone** when the microwave is switched off. Let it stand for 4-5 minutes. It becomes alright & turns dry on standing.
- Let cake cool 5-10 minutes before removing from the baking dish.
- Microwaved cakes taste better if eaten after a few hours. They might appear a little moist if eaten immediately.
- Baking dish should only be filled 3/4 to allow room for cake to rise.

Chocolate Walnut Cake

A quick microwaved eggless chocolate cake.
Picture on page 84

Serves 6

9" ROUND DEEP BOWL

½ tin condensed milk (milk-maid)
½ cup milk, ½ cup (75 gm) butter, preferably unsalted
1½ tbsp powdered sugar
100 gms (1 cup) maida (plain flour)
¼ cup cocoa
¾ tsp level soda-bi-carb (mitha soda)
¾ tsp level baking powder
½ tsp vanilla essence
2 tbsp finely chopped walnuts

1. Sift maida with cocoa, soda-bicarb and baking powder. Keep aside.
2. Mix sugar and butter. Beat till very fluffy. Add milk-maid. Beat well.
3. Add milk and essence. Add maida. Beat well for 3-4 minutes till the mixture is smooth and light.
4. Add walnuts. Mix well. Transfer to a big, greased deep dish of 9" diameter.
5. **Microwave for 5 minutes**. Let it cool.
6. **Let it stand for 4-5 minutes**.
7. Let it cool for 5-10 minutes before removing from baking dish.
8. Serve after a little while.

Basic Vanilla Cake

Serves 4-5

8-9" ROUND ALUMINIUM CAKE TIN
THIS CAKE IS FOR THE CONVECTION MODE

½ tin condensed milk (milk-maid)
½ cup milk, ½ cup (75 gm) butter
1½ tbsp powdered sugar
125 gms (1¼ cup) maida (plain flour)
¾ tsp level soda-bi-carb, ¾ tsp level baking powder
1 tsp vanilla essence

1. Sift maida with soda-bi-carb and baking powder. Keep aside.
2. Mix sugar and butter. Beat till very fluffy. Add milk-maid. Beat well.
3. Add milk and essence. Add maida. Beat well for 3-4 minutes till the mixture is smooth and light. Transfer to a big greased 9" diameter round aluminium cake tin.
4. Preheat oven to 150°C by using the convec mode. Put the cake tin on the grill rack and bake at 150°C for 45 minutes. Remove from oven after 5 minutes.